# MEGA MACHINES!

# AMAZING AIRCRAFT CARRIERS

## BY NATALIE HUMPHREY

Gareth Stevens
PUBLISHING

**Please visit our website, www.garethstevens.com. For a free color catalog of all our high-quality books, call toll free 1-800-542-2595 or fax 1-877-542-2596.**

Portions of this work were originally authored by Kenny Allen and published as *Aircraft Carriers*. All new material in this edition is authored by Natalie Humphrey.

**Cataloging-in-Publication Data**

Names: Humphrey, Natalie.
Title: Amazing aircraft carriers / Natalie Humphrey.
Description: New York : Gareth Stevens Publishing, 2023. | Series: Mega machines! | Includes glossary and index.
Identifiers: ISBN 9781538282991 (pbk.) | ISBN 9781538283011 (library bound) | ISBN 9781538283028 (ebook)
Subjects: LCSH: Aircraft carriers–Juvenile literature.
Classification: LCC V874.H86 2023 | DDC 623.825'5–dc23

Published in 2023 by
**Gareth Stevens Publishing**
2455 Clinton Street
Buffalo, NY 14224

Designer: Deanna Paternostro
Editor: Natalie Humphrey

Photo credits: Cover, p. 1 Video Media Studio Europe/Shutterstock.com; pp. 3, 4, 6, 8, 10, 12, 14, 16, 18, 20, 21 (bottom), 22, 23, 24 Nataliia K/Shutterstock.com; p. 5 GreenOak/Shutterstock.com; p. 7 Claudine Van Massenhove/Shutterstock.com; p. 9 vanchai tan/Shutterstock.com; p. 11 BeAvPhoto/Shutterstock.com; p. 13 schusterbauer.com/Shutterstock.com; p. 15 Guillermo Pis Gonzalez/Shutterstock.com; p. 17 Fœ/Wikimedia Commons; p. 19 Derek Gordon/Shutterstock.com; p. 21 (top) Avigator Fortuner/Shutterstock.com.

Printed in the United States of America

Some of the images in this book illustrate individuals who are models. The depictions do not imply actual situations or events.

CPSIA compliance information: Batch #CW23GS: For further information contact Gareth Stevens at 1-800-542-2595.

Find us on

# CONTENTS

**Boldface** words appear in the glossary.

# Mega Ship

An aircraft carrier is one **massive** machine! This huge ship can be almost as long as four football fields and can carry around 5,000 **personnel** at the same time. The largest aircraft carrier can hold more than 75 U.S. Navy aircraft!

# Made of Steel

Aircraft carriers are very heavy.
They are made from thick steel
to help keep the ship's crew safe.
The top is very wide, but the part
under the water is much narrower.
Inside there are about 25 levels,
called decks.

# Time for Takeoff!

Jets take off and land on a long, flat strip on top of the aircraft carrier. This area is called the flight deck. Many **military** members work together on the flight deck. Some make sure pilots stay safe. Pilots are people who fly planes.

# Catapults and Cables

Officers on the aircraft carrier need to help jets take off and land. During takeoffs, **catapults** help the jets get up to speed very quickly. When landing, jets have hooks that grab onto strong cables to slow them down quickly.

# Lookout

The command center of an aircraft carrier is called an island. Officers in the island watch flights take off and land. Other military members steer the ship. **Radar** dishes on the island help the crew find enemies. Radio **antennas** allow officers to talk to pilots.

## Jet Storage

Jets are stored below deck in a large space called the hangar. Several giant elevators move jets between the hangar and the flight deck. Aircraft carriers also carry helicopters. These are aircraft with metal blades on top that turn around a center point.

## Floating Cities

Aircraft carriers are so big, they are like floating cities! Navy sailors often live and work on the middle decks. Those decks may have a post office, hospital, basketball court, and stores. Aircraft carriers even have their own newspapers and TV studios!

# Powerful Propellers

Aircraft carriers use special power to get moving. Many aircraft carriers use **engines** with four **propellers** powered by **nuclear energy**. These engines are on the lowest deck. They create so much energy they could power 12,000 homes! This energy powers the ship's lights and machinery.

## Life at Sea

Aircraft carriers don't need to dock very often. They can stay at sea for about 25 years without refueling! When aircraft carriers need to be repaired, or fixed, they go to giant docks. The navy has around 18 docks where aircraft carriers can go.

**Mega Machine Facts:** Nimitz class Aircraft Carriers

**Length:** 1,092 feet (332.85 m)

**Weight:** 110,000 tons (99,000 mt)

**Speed:** 34.5 miles (55.5 km) per hour or more

**Cost:** $8.5 billion

# GLOSSARY

**antenna:** A metal rod used to send and receive radio messages.

**catapult:** A machine that throws something with great force.

**engine:** A machine that makes power.

**massive:** Very big and often heavy.

**military:** Having to do with armed forces.

**nuclear energy:** Energy created by using tiny pieces of matter called atoms.

**personnel:** A group of people who work at a place.

**propeller:** Paddle-like parts on a ship that spin in the water to move the ship forward.

**radar:** A way of using radio waves to find distant objects.

# FOR MORE INFORMATION

## BOOKS

Rajczak, Michael. *How to Build an Aircraft Carrier*. New York, NY: Gareth Stevens Publishing, 2021.

Ransom, Candice F. *How Aircraft Carriers Work*. Minneapolis, MN: Lerner Publications, 2020.

## WEBSITES

**Britannica Kids**
*kids.britannica.com/kids/article/navy/353522*
Learn more about the U.S. Navy and its aircraft carriers!

**Intrepid Museum**
*www.intrepidmuseum.org/education*
Find out more about aircraft carriers on board the retired *Intrepid* aircraft carrier!

# INDEX